MY MIND WON'T SHUT UP!

**Meditation For People
Who Don't Meditate**

TRIGGER™
The mental health & wellbeing publisher

ABOUT THE AUTHORS

We're sisters, sturdy-legged bacon-sandwich-munching Glaswegians. We looked for real-life stuff about meditation that would appeal to ordinary people like us, with money worries, difficult families and haemorrhoids – but we couldn't find much.

So we wrote this.

Marion Williamson is an author and editor. This is her fourth book. She edited *Prediction* magazine for ten years and writes for oodles of different magazines and websites. See more at: www.marionwilliamson.com

Linda Williamson is an IT project manager for the NHS in London. She's obsessed with meditation books, retreats and classes but despite this, she still regularly manages to lock herself out of her flat.

ABOUT THE ILLUSTRATOR

For the last 15 years Rosie Balyuzi has freelanced in graphic design and illustration. Most recently, she illustrated *Simplify: How to Stay Sane in a World Going Mad* (Watkins, 2020). She offers great little snippets of life advice on her Instagram: @doodlesurfer

MY MIND WON'T SHUT UP!

Meditation For People Who Don't Meditate

By Linda and Marion Williamson

Illustrations by Rosie Balyuzi

TRIGGER
The mental health & wellbeing publisher

First published in 2021
This edition published in 2023 by Trigger Publishing
An imprint of Shaw Callaghan Ltd

UK Office
The Stanley Building
7 Pancras Square
Kings Cross
London N1C 4AG

US Office
On Point Executive Center, Inc
3030 N Rocky Point Drive W
Suite 150
Tampa, FL 33607
www.triggerhub.org

A CIP catalogue record for this book is available
upon request from the British Library
ISBN: 978-1-83796-276-1
Ebook ISBN: 978-1-83796-277-8

Cover design by Design Marque
Typeset by JCS Publishing Services Ltd

DEDICATION

This book is dedicated to our friend Ross. When we mentioned we were writing a book on meditation, Ross said, "I vaguely feel I should be doing something about my mind, but I'm not sure what." This inspired us. We thought if we could encourage Ross to meditate, we were on the right path.

CONTENTS

A NOTE FROM THE AUTHORS

What this book is . . .

○ It's what you need to know about meditation, without being too earnest.

○ We squish myths about meditation being all pan pipes and incense.

○ We'll show you how to manage your preposterously messy brain, making you feel a bit happier and more in control.

○ The book tackles all your wriggly excuses that discourage you from making meditation a habit.

What this book isn't . . .

○ This book is not a spiritual journey.

○ We can't show you how to control your thoughts and feelings – having a chaotic mind is just an annoying part of being human.

○ There's nothing religious in here.

○ It won't make you better at Kung Fu.

INTRODUCTION

The problem with the word 'meditation' is that it carries so much woo-woo baggage. You don't have to be interested in clean-living, mantras or attaining oneness with the Universe to find meditation helpful. Simply put, meditation is being aware of your thoughts, emotions and senses in the present moment. After meditating for a few moments, you'll be astonished at the turmoil inside your mind. This is everyone's experience. If you take one thing from this book it should be this: the whole point of meditating is noticing that your mind won't shut up.

"The whole point of meditating is noticing that your mind won't shut up"

Meditation shows you that most of your thinking is ludicrously unhelpful. You'll quickly discover you're giving yourself terrible advice and being viciously unpleasant to yourself. The more you're aware of your repetitive internal gibberish, the easier it will be to spot unhelpful thoughts, drop them or replace them with kinder ones. This applies to everyone's minds – even you, with your weird obsessions, insecurities and fantasies.

There's impressive neuroscience evidence confirming what people have known for centuries: meditating for just a few minutes a day will make you happier, calmer and better in bed (kidding!). So you'll still be you, but with your shit together.

CHAPTER 1

What Your Mind Does . . . and Why Meditation Helps

**"It's one of those
'simple but not easy' things."**

Relax, everyone has a voice in their head that never shuts up!

Your mind talks rubbish! Have you ever really listened to what's going on in there? It's chaos. You're anxious about a sulking partner, angry at the traffic and confused about your friend being weird at lunch. Money problems make you panic and you feel guilty about what you said to your mum four years ago. In any one minute there's endless repetition, planning and fantasies.

You make ceaseless associations and ping off on weird tangents, fragmenting your energy and getting nowhere. Your memory skips back in time and leaps into the future but you're never really *here*. How can you trust your mind when it's like this? And who is actually in charge?

Face it, you're a chimp!

Biologically, you're a problem-solving monkey. Evolution has given you a nervous system that's constantly on edge, scanning the horizon for possible threats and rewards. The world around you has changed exponentially but your brain hasn't evolved beyond spearing antelopes on the savanna. You're using old equipment to cope with a far weirder and more complex world than your brain was designed to handle. Your hyper-switched-on nervous system is skilled at defending against unexpected dinosaurs but it's not so useful when you explode with rage because your flight has been cancelled. Evolution doesn't want you to be content. Content = complacent = eaten by wild dogs.

"There's no end to what we can find to worry about"

Our minds evolved to solve problems, and this enabled us chimps to take over the world! Identifying threats is what our minds like to do best, but in our modern information-loaded environment this means there is no end to what we can find to worry about. It's a bit like when you're on holiday: everything's sorted at the office, your cat's being fed, you're lying on a sun-lounger with an ice cream, but you can't rest until you've booked your return transfer to the airport.

"Your brain doesn't make you happy – its purpose is to keep you alive!"

A part of you is convinced that if you solve all your problems you'll feel at peace. The difficulty is that your brain is designed to find new stuff to worry about. If you don't have any obvious or immediate problems, you can be sure you'll find something to get nervous about soon. Your brain was not designed to make you happy – its purpose is to keep you alive!

Extreme entertainment

Our monkey minds weren't meant to deal with the extremes of stimulation and distraction that are now available to us. We're overwhelmed by the vast information-creating vortex of the Internet. The 24-hour rolling news reminds you of dangers the world over. Addictive gaming, productivity tools and messaging apps scream for your attention. Sophisticated advertising hijacks you daily, reminding you that you're bald, old and your house is filthy.

"Gaming, gambling and porn sounds like brilliant fun but it's actually draining and addictive"

It's increasingly hard to switch off. You read work emails instead of enjoying your courgette frittata and send out delusional tweets when you should be focused on being the President of the USA. Instant access to entertainment, gambling and pornography sounds like it should be brilliant, but actually it's addictive and unsatisfying.

The tsunami of distraction means it's harder to focus than when we were living a simple but dangerous life in a cave. All these confusing and contradictory pressures leave you feeling exhausted, alienated and fat.

What is meditation?

In the simplest terms, meditation is being able to notice your thoughts without getting caught up in them. When you meditate you ring-fence time to practise a mental skill. Meditation techniques help you understand what's going on with your mind and make you appreciate the magic of being in the present moment.

"You'll learn how to gently focus (meditate) on one thing"

You'll learn how to gently focus (meditate) on one thing. This can be your breathing, sounds, other people or the tingle in your toes (these focal points are called 'anchors'). When you notice your thoughts trying to take over, you just return to your anchor. It's one of those 'simple but not easy' things because within moments of trying to meditate, everyone finds themselves getting carried away by their thinking.

"It's not all about people in expensive yoga clothes eating lots of kale"

What meditation isn't

It's not serene-looking people draped in expensive yoga gear offering comforting-sounding, banal advice like: "Listen with an awakened heart", "Radiating awareness" and "Eat lots of kale". If you Google 'meditation' you'll arrive in a world very different to the one you currently inhabit – an airbrushed universe awash with soothing pan pipes, soft candlelight and trickling water features. The bracing reality is that when you meditate you'll be plonked right in the heart of your own life, exactly as it is – suck it up!

MEDITATION VERSUS MINDFULNESS

The terms 'mindfulness' and 'meditation' are often bandied about and intermingled, but they aren't the same thing. Mindfulness is when you're paying careful attention to something and meditation is when you're practising a mental technique. You can drink a cup of tea mindfully, listening to the water being poured, noticing the steam rising from the cup, enjoying how the tea is brewed and appreciating the taste. By all means do things mindfully! It's fantastically helpful to focus intently on what's going on around you in the present moment. It's also very soothing if you're feeling anxious, as it takes your attention away from your thoughts and back to your senses.

If you were meditating on making a cup of tea you would be trying to concentrate on one tea-making aspect. This might be the steam rising from the cup, bringing your attention back to it whenever your mind wanders.

The term 'mindful meditation' is often used to describe a common type of meditation that we have decided to name 'Single Focus meditation' to avoid confusion.

ALL CHANGE

Buddha says, "Everything changes." You know this is true but how good are you at applying it to your everyday life? Change makes the world unreliable. You shouldn't expect to get lasting happiness from something unstable – ask anyone who has dated Boris Johnson.* One of the insights of meditation is to see that your world is always changing: your thoughts, emotions and physical sensations are in constant flux. Although this could seem negative, it's actually a gift. Buddhists believe that really understanding that everything changes (like in your bones understanding it, not just on an intellectual level) releases you from suffering.

Saying, "This too shall pass" should be applied whether you're having a wonderful seaside picnic or faking an orgasm. Once you accept that nothing ever stays as it is, change becomes less of a problem. You accept the truth of it and stop picking a fight with reality.

*Or someone equally as unreliable.

The science of meditation

You know you're on to something when meditation is adopted by the police, air force and the military. Neuroscience studies show that meditating re-wires your brain. Harvard scientists Dr Daniel Goleman and Dr Richard J Davidson wanted to see if long-term meditating affects the amygdala – an area of your brain associated with 'fight or flight' reactions. Their research showed activity in the amygdala is reduced when you meditate, and a long-term practise improves your ability to handle stress in a more permanent way.

"Neuroscience studies
show that meditating
re-wires your brain"

The scientists also studied the Olympic athletes of meditation – Buddhist monks who had been meditating over eight hours a day for years. Their amygdalas were super calm when they were meditating, and these changes continued even when they weren't meditating.

Meditation is also helpful in managing pain. Dr Jon Kabat-Zinn ran a clinic in the USA called the Mindfulness-Based Stress Reduction Program that taught patients suffering with chronic pain how to meditate for eight weeks. The results show meditation lessens the emotional side of pain. The pain itself does not go away but the anxiety associated with it reduces. Research scientists at UC Davis University in California also found that meditation lowers the amount of the stress hormone, cortisol.

Most researchers would agree that more studies are needed but there is growing evidence that regular meditation changes your brain in a positive way. In the next chapter we'll show you how to get started so you can get straight to the goodies. But first let's look at some of the benefits of meditation.

NINE INSPIRING BENEFITS

Here's Why You Bought This Book...

1
YOU'LL BE CALMER AND HAPPIER

Meditation teaches you to be still, to accept what is. You can learn to be okay with what's happening in your life right now, even if you spent 20 minutes hiding in the office toilets this morning. Meditating ups your happy quota by teaching you that life is only made up of moments. When you're not worrying about the past or future you can enjoy being here in the present.

"Meditation teaches you that you don't have to give every unhappy thought too much importance"

2
YOU'LL STOP FREAKING OUT SO MUCH!

Meditation makes you more aware of what your mind is up to. Most of the time you are lost in thought – it's like having your own YouTube channel, playing associated clips, one after the other. Meditation skills give you the ability to pop yourself out of your thought bubble and get back some control. For example, say you are filling out a job application form and the deadline is this afternoon. You're getting stressed and you're thinking along the lines of, "Shit, I've only got two hours to complete this, I will never do it in time. I will never get another job. What if I become homeless? I'd be on the streets. I could get ill and rats would gnaw my legs to stumps." This is a perfectly ordinary thought process . . . but it's not helpful.

With practice, you'll see when your thoughts have run away with themselves. This helps you decide if you want to continue with the homeless disaster scenario or whether, like a loveable idiot, you realize you got distracted and decide to get on with the job application.

"You'll see when your thoughts have run away with themselves"

3
YOU'LL DISCOVER YOUR OFF SWITCH

Having loads on your mind is exhausting. If you're angry, stressed or over-excited, meditation stops you sifting through events and conversations, giving you a breather. When your thoughts are cantering you lose sight of what's important. This ability to drop the internal dialogue is a sanity-saving skill.

"Cantering thoughts makes you lose sight of what's important"

4
YOU'LL CREATE TIME THAT'S JUST FOR YOU

Most of us have multiple roles to play in our lives. You may be a parent, boss, fetish party organizer and a member of the Panda Appreciation Society. All of these duties come with perfectly reasonable demands and obligations, but they can be incessant and often conflict. Meditation is an expectation-free zone. Nobody will ask you to achieve anything or demand you be witty or informed about the UN carbon emissions targets. This can be a huge relief. A small demands-free oasis in your day is refreshing and you will be taking care of yourself in a practical, tangible way.

"Nobody will expect you
to be witty"

5
YOU'LL BE NICER TO OTHER PEOPLE

cafe

When you appreciate that everyone has to deal with their own low-level of madness, you become a bit kinder to them. Your worst behaviour comes out when you are burning with difficult emotions such as anger, jealousy and anxiety. Meditation makes you happier, so if you are feeling good, you'll be nicer to people.

Our culture encourages us to be self-centred but trying to manipulate the world into making you happy doesn't work. The world isn't interested in meeting your needs. But if you focus on other people's wellbeing – buy someone a coffee or make them smile – it stops being all about you and your stupid shit. What a relief!

"It stops being all about you and your stupid shit"

6

MEDITATION HELPS YOU IDENTIFY AND CHANGE BAD MENTAL HABITS

Meditation helps you get to know yourself a bit better. You'll identify the mental habits that aren't doing you much good, such as: worrying, getting stuff out of proportion, obsessing, or maybe you're habitually angry, always checking for the latest person who pissed you off. You'll also become more aware of the emotions causing these negative habits – the fear, anger, desire and need for excitement. With practice, you'll feel more able to cope with these insistent little monsters when they take hold. Meditation won't eliminate all your anxieties, they're just part of being human. But it will help you spot when you repeat the same pattern, so you can give yourself a break.

"You'll identify the mental habits that aren't doing you much good"

7
YOU'LL BUILD MENTAL AND EMOTIONAL RESILIENCE

One of the biggest benefits of meditation is that it gives you tools to tackle anything that comes your way. You are training your mind to respond to all situations. There's a full smorgasbord of problems that can hit your life: career disasters, heartbreak, haemorrhoids, grief and of course the ever-present possibility of death! Everyone has to deal with these at some point and no amount of planning, worrying or bargaining will avoid them completely. It can be oddly liberating to recognize that. Meditation cuts to the chase by helping you deal with exactly what you've got in front of you, right now.

Even if you don't have any major issues at the moment, meditating regularly gives you an advantage when the tough stuff hits – you'll have a bunch of mental tools up your sleeves, ready to put into action.

"Meditation cuts to the chase by helping you deal with exactly what you've got in front of you"

8
YOU'LL FEEL MORE CONNECTED TO YOUR BODY

Because you're usually caught up in your thoughts, most of the time you're not listening to your body and you ignore what it's trying to tell you. Meditation encourages you to focus on how you are feeling, rather than what you are thinking. All your emotions are experienced in your body, that's why they're called feelings. You know you're experiencing rage or jealousy because your body reacts in such a visceral way.

Focusing on the physical sensations caused by your emotions stops you thinking about the story that triggered them. This gives you time to calm down and allows your emotions to run their course. Repressing your emotions only means they'll come out in some other way. Meditation provides a safe space where you can discharge some of the intensity of what you're experiencing.

"Focus on how you are feeling, rather than what you are thinking"

9
YOU'LL APPRECIATE THAT YOUR LIFE IS HAPPENING RIGHT NOW

It's a strangely over-looked fact of human experience that you only ever live the present moment and only ever will. Meditation reminds you that all you have is 'now'. Your memories and plans are all thoughts completed in the present. Yet how often are you actually aware of now? You miss enjoying your cup of tea because you're worried about a tricky conversation you need to have at work in four days' time. You can get so lost in trying to re-write the past that you miss what's good about the present. Don't spend all your time trying to get to the next thing. Your life is mostly made up of the stuff in-between your plans. Meditation teaches you to relax and appreciate all the moments that make up your life.

"'This too shall pass' applies whether you're having a picnic or faking an orgasm"

CHAPTER 2

How to Meditate

"As soon as you try to meditate you'll notice that your brain will not shut up. This happens because you are human, and humans think all the goddam time."

Where, when and for how long?

First, locate your heart chakra and an incense burner. We're joking – it's actually very simple. Find somewhere you won't be interrupted, ideally a place where you feel safe and relaxed.

"You're picturing the cross-legged
lotus position, aren't you?"

That could be on your sofa, on a chair in the kitchen or sitting on the toilet if that's where you feel most comfortable. Some people make a little space in a corner of a room. Others go the whole hog and build an altar with candles, incense, herbal tea and kittens – that's all fine too, but definitely not necessary. There isn't a prescriptive amount of time to meditate. To feel the benefits, you're looking at about five to ten minutes a day. But if that's too much, even one minute will help. Try not to give yourself an unrealistic target. A timer is helpful for this but keep the ring-tone tranquil – it's jarring to be yanked out of your quiet time by a 'Crazy Frog' alarm.

Identify when you've got ten minutes of uninterrupted time. Mornings are good as you don't have to deal with the guilt of, "Oh fuck, I've still not meditated" as the day goes on. Or if you've got kids and its impossible while getting them all off to school, meditate for five minutes when they're gone, while the house is calm. Before you go to bed is fine, but you might be tempted to sleep through it. We're big fans of hiding in toilets – you can take five minutes to yourself and it's impolite to be asked what you were doing!

"Oh fuck, I've still not meditated"

Posture

You're picturing the cross-legged lotus position, aren't you? Unless you're super-bendy and comfortable like that, forget it. All you need is an ordinary comfortable seated position for the duration of your session. This can be on the floor or on a chair. Your spine should be straight but not rigid – relaxed but alert is what you're aiming for – stable and supported rather than too mushy. Lying down isn't recommended because it's hard not to doze off.

Ideally, you're looking for a straight-backed chair that gives you a bit of support, with your feet on the ground. You might want a cushion on your lap because your arms can feel quite heavy and pull you forward after a while, so this gives somewhere to rest them. If you have any sore spots or injuries, just adapt your position until you're comfortable. You can buy a custom-made meditation cushion. These are less squishy than regular ones and are designed to support your body. You don't have to close your eyes when meditating but it can help you focus.

"A slight smile can help relax your face but if it feels weird, don't worry about it"

Set your intention

To prepare for meditation have a quick scan of how you're feeling. Is your jaw clenched? Are your shoulders up by your ears? Are you anxious? Pissed off? Chirpy? Note where you're holding tension and release it if you can. A slight smile can help relax your face but if it feels weird, don't worry about it. Before you start, set a positive intention for the session – such as, "I will focus on my breathing."

"You're not aiming for any weird 'spiritual' breathing"

Simple breathing meditation

Now you're going to try a simple Single Focus meditation. The easiest thing to concentrate on is usually your breath because (hopefully) it's always available. You don't have to breathe in any particular way. You're not aiming for deep breathing or any weird 'spiritual' breathing, just notice how your normal breath feels to you right now. You don't need to change it. Focusing on one thing is often described as having an 'anchor' as it steadies you and gathers your attention.

○ Pay attention to the sensations created by breathing in and breathing out, one breath at a time. Notice where the sensation is strongest: is it in the rise and fall of your belly, through your nose or the top of your lip? The point is to feel the breathing process, not to describe it to yourself or think about it.

"You'll get distracted by your thinking but this is what meditation is"

○ This leads us to what will almost immediately happen – you're going to get distracted by your thinking. But this is what meditation is. Just notice it and return your concentration to feeling your breath. Being aware that you got distracted and going back to what you wanted to focus on is the whole point. That's the heavy lifting of the meditation exercise.

"Don't beat yourself up about getting distracted – that just makes you more distracted"

○ You will probably get interrupted by your thoughts for most of the five minutes. Don't beat yourself up about this, that just adds to being distracted. Just gently notice when you get caught in your thoughts, then start again with feeling the breath. Do this until the timer pings, open your eyes if they were closed, and get on with your day. You did it – we'll mail you your pan pipes!

"Expectations of instant calmness set you up for a kicking"

Read this when you finish

As soon as you try to meditate you'll notice that your brain will not shut up. This happens because you are human, and humans think all the goddam time. Even Tibetan monks brought up in monasteries are constantly distracted by their thoughts. Nothing will stop your restless monkey-mind from thinking.

Within seconds of closing your eyes you were probably wondering if you were meditating yet and if your posture was right, you might have been wriggling a bit and feeling self-conscious. The fact that you've noticed that you're thinking means you're doing it right. Making a start is the hardest part of all. Give yourself a high five.

I can't do it!

There's no such thing as being 'bad' at meditation. The good news is that if you're following your breath (or whatever you've chosen as your anchor) and coming back to it when you get distracted, you're meditating. Spotting your tendency to doubt yourself is actually quite an advanced sign that you're becoming more aware of your mental habits, so you're doing well. Try not to set goals for yourself like: "I'm going to have three minutes of complete stillness". Expectations of instant calmness set you up for a kicking. Be nice to yourself, you idiot!

NOT ALL THOUGHTS ARE TROUBLE

Thinking is essential – you have to plan, analyse and think creatively to live your life. What meditation makes clear is the sheer tonnage of unhelpful thoughts that come along with the good stuff. In meditation circles, thinking sometimes gets a bad rap. Of course you need to think so you can get stuff done, but endless repetition, worrying and negative self-talk just isn't that helpful.

Breathe normally

When you first start noticing your breath in meditation, you might find that your breathing changes a bit, almost like you're trying to do it better. There isn't anything special about your breathing, it's just a constant, neutral thing to focus on. You don't need to breathe deeply or from the diaphragm. Sometimes people can become so tightly focused, they stop breathing altogether! Relax and breathe like you normally do. If focusing on breathing makes you feel uncomfortable for any reason, we offer other alternatives in Chapter 3.

> "There isn't anything special about your breathing, it's just a constant, neutral thing to focus on"

Also, some people find it helpful to close their eyes when they meditate as it can tune out distractions. But it can freak other people out. Either is fine. If you keep them open, maybe keep a soft focus on a spot in front of you. Try not to get too absorbed in how much you like your new fluffy rug.

IS IT WORKING?

How do you know if meditation is helping? If you expected instant peace to descend in your session, and instead you're just you with all your usual shit, you might think you're doing it wrong. Our suggestion is that how your latest meditation session goes isn't the best way to measure whether it's working or not. A better indicator would be an improvement in your day-to-day life. Do you feel more present? Lighter, maybe? Nicer to people? A little calmer or less distracted? Then it's working.

"Do you feel more present?
Lighter, maybe?"

Watching the washing machine

Tim Ferriss, productivity guru and author of *The 4-Hour Work Week*, noted that meditation is a bit like watching a washing machine. Imagine your thoughts are the clothes inside, tumbling and sloshing about and you're watching it – just noticing at a bit of a distance – and not getting too involved in your thoughts.

CHAPTER 3

Oodles of Meditation Options

"You can meditate on anything from the warmth in your hands to the humming sound of your fridge."

Don't be scared, there are are plenty of types of meditation

There are heaps of ways to approach meditation. Give them all a shot, keep the ones that work for you and don't worry about the rest. One method isn't better than the others, but have an open mind about the types that don't immediately appeal, as they may work for you later on. If any of them make you recoil in horror, then there's probably something in there that needs to be explored!

Four Single Focus meditations

Single Focus meditations are when you place your attention on one thing. As mentioned in the introduction, your anchor could be your breath, walking, a tree or sound. What you choose to meditate on is not special, it is the quality of your attention that matters. When you get used to the idea and have tried a few Single Focus techniques, you can meditate on anything from the warmth in your hands to the humming sound of your fridge. You're aiming for a kind of friendly openness that accepts the present moment just as it is. By returning to your anchor again and again, you are cultivating concentration and clarity. Try these four types and see which works best:

1

Single Focus meditation: Breathing

This is the breathing exercise covered in the last chapter. You just focus on your breath and when you get distracted, come back to it again. No incense, mantras or whale songs required.

"No incense, mantras or whale songs required"

2

Single Focus meditation: Walking

Sometimes sitting with your eyes closed can make your emotions loom too near the surface, or maybe you just feel too restless to keep still. Walking meditation builds concentration and awareness – and you can move around. This method centres on how your body feels as you move, always returning to this when you get distracted. The idea is to feel the sensations of walking rather than thinking about them.

"Important safety tip – steer clear of cliffs and ponds"

- The first time you try walking meditation, set a timer for five minutes and, as usual, start with an intention – "I'm going to focus on my feet" is fine. It's up to you whether your shoes are on or off, whether you're inside your house or in a field of alpacas. Important safety tip – keep your eyes open and stay clear of cliffs and ponds. Start by walking as you usually do, at a normal pace. Then maybe slow it down a little.

- Really feel the movement of each step. Focus on what it's like to lift your foot up, move your leg forward and step it down. Get interested in the feeling of each step, one at a time. Up, move, step. Up, move, step. It might be hard to keep up with your physical actions at first, but try to notice the subtle details. Where does your foot land when it touches the ground? On the ball of your foot? On the heel? What is the sense of pressure like? How does your sock feel? Smooth? A bit scratchy? What's the temperature like in your feet? Warm? Is it different in each foot? Maybe your toes are cold but the front of your foot is warm?

"Make sure you're not doing it grimly, through gritted teeth"

- Can you notice the way you adjust the weight in your foot? Feel all the sensations of your legs and feet. When you get distracted from the feeling of walking (and you will almost immediately) just guide your focus back to your feet. Relax and walk comfortably, enjoy the simplicity of just walking. Make sure you're not doing it grimly, through gritted teeth. Maybe you fancy imitating a velociraptor. That's all cool, but really keep your focus on how it feels to walk like a velociraptor.

- Keep up the attentive walking until the timer sounds. Once you get the hang of it, you can walk at your normal pace if that feels okay. Walking meditation means you can sneak more meditation into your day without finding extra time. Walking to the bus, between meetings and up the stairs are all useful options.

3

Single Focus meditation: Sound

This is a very simple way of meditating and it gives you a refreshing break from your inner monologue. This meditation works anywhere: walking to work, doing the dishes, gardening or having a pee. Sound meditation is really easy to stuff into small pockets of time in your day.

"This works anywhere – walking to work, gardening or having a pee"

- Switch on your timer for five minutes and begin by setting your intention. Sometimes it's difficult to remember what you're meant to be doing, so saying to yourself, "I'll focus on the sounds of the park", for example, will help.

- Close your eyes and sit in a relaxed but alert way. Take a few breaths and settle into your body then move your focus to what you can hear.

- Pay close attention. You might hear the traffic, birds, a plane, a radiator clicking or a moment of silence. Just keep centred on the rising and falling of the sounds.

- When you catch yourself thinking, don't get all judgmental about it; come back to just listening. Try not to get caught up in describing sounds to yourself. Just notice what you hear. Then when the timer goes off, that's you finished.

4

Single Focus meditation: Body Scan

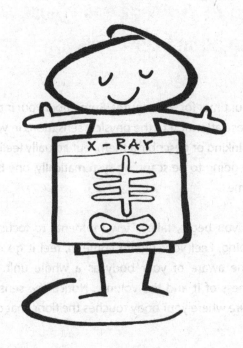

As you might have guessed, body scan meditation uses the physical sensations of your body as your anchor. Most of the time, you ignore what's happening below your own neck. This meditation reminds you to connect with your body, just as it is. You can try this sitting in a comfortable chair or lying down.

Your posture should be relaxed but alert. Your eyes can be open or closed, either is fine, but if you are lying down with your eyes shut, you might end up snoring.

"Most of the time you ignore what's happening below your own neck"

- Set your timer for ten minutes. Remember your intention to pay close attention to the physical sensations in your body, not thinking or describing them, but actually feeling them. You're going to be scanning systematically, one body part at a time.

- When you begin, take a few moments to focus on your breathing. Feel your breath come in, feel it go out. Then become aware of your body as a whole unit. Feel the heaviness of it and the volume. Notice the sensations of pressure where your body touches the floor, mat or chair.

"You don't have to wiggle your toes to create a feeling"

- Then start to move your awareness to your left foot and toes. What can you feel? Tingling? Warmth? What's the temperature like? Maybe there is no sensation – that's fine, just note it and move on. You don't have to wiggle your toes to create a feeling. Just notice what's going on with your toes.

- Then move up to your shin. What's it like there? Is there a feeling of your skin touching your clothes? Maybe an ache? Coolness?

- Then move on to your knee, with the same enquiry. Treat each part of your body with the same openness and kindness until you reach the top of your head. You don't need to worry about the exact order you do this in as long you cover your whole body. It doesn't matter if you don't have any sensations in some bits of your body, that's quite normal.

- Remember you are not trying to summon a particular feeling, you're just being open to what's going on. If you get distracted, and of course you will, just return to your body scan.

- When the timer pings, you're done!

Three Positive Connection meditations

Positive Connection meditations are different to the Single Focus methods because you'll be concentrating on feeling connected to yourself, others and, at the end, the whole planet! The purpose of these meditations is to improve your relationship with yourself and others, making you more compassionate and generally less snarky.

If you need more convincing that this could be helpful, imagine if you woke up in a hideous mood and spent ten minutes intensely thinking about what you hated most about yourself and everyone else. Really get into the specifics of what you find upsetting and inflame the sore points. Would this colour your day and affect how you interact with people? Damn right it would! The opposite is also true. Thinking of people in a kind way isn't so much for their benefit – it's for yours!

"This should be an irony-free zone, which takes courage"

This type of meditation involves repeating phrases that affirm your good wishes for yourself and others. Don't get too caught up in finding the perfect words, it's the intention to wish people well that's key. Watch for an ironic tone creeping in: "May BMW drivers discover how to signal before overtaking" is pleasingly sarcastic but not helpful. This should be an irony-free zone, which takes courage. Give the following three meditations a try and see how it goes.

1

Positive Connection meditation:
Friendliness for all

This meditation is split into five parts, each concentrating on sending positive thoughts: to yourself, a friend, a neutral person, someone you find annoying and, lastly, all living things. It takes ten minutes – two minutes each for five parts. Set your timer. Find a space where you won't be interrupted and sit relaxed and alert.

> "It helps if you don't have the hots for the person you're thinking of so you don't get side-tracked"

● *You (two minutes)*
  Think of yourself and say (in your mind) the phrases you have chosen, such as, "May I be well, may I be happy" or "I wish myself to be safe and loved." It can be anything you like as long as it resonates with you. Just repeating words like 'kindness' or 'happiness' is fine, but try to really connect with the meaning of the words. Avoid lottery-winning wishes or intentions that veer away from simple goodwill. You might need to remind yourself of your intention to

meditate sincerely and find phrases that don't make you cringe. It's easier if you use the same words for each of the five parts so you don't have to remember new ones for each person. Repeat the phrases for two minutes, then move on to the next.

- **Close friend (two minutes)**
Bring to mind a friend you care about. It helps if you don't have the hots for them, as it's easy to get side-tracked. Repeat your chosen phrases for two minutes, remembering a kindness or something you like about them. Visualize them being happy, for example, or that time they laughed so hard beer came out their nose – whatever allows you to feel connected to your friend.

- **Neutral person (two minutes)**
This should be someone you're on nodding terms with but don't know that well. The person that serves your coffee? The quiet guy who's always on the rowing machine at the gym or the woman you see walking her dog in the morning would all be good examples. Repeat your phrases for two minutes. It may be tricky to stay linked to the person because you don't have much to go on. Your mind might waver and make up stories about them but just come back to your intention to send them good wishes.

"Don't focus on a person who spews up a lava of hatred – that's for advanced meditators"

- **Difficult person (two minutes)**

  Choose someone tedious or who pisses you off. Don't focus on a person who spews up a lava of hatred – that's for advanced meditators. This isn't going to be easy because soon you will get sucked into the story of why you dislike them. Be aware of this and just return to repeating the phrases, doing your best to connect with the person and wish them well.

- **All living things (two minutes)**

  Yep, that's everything that's alive, including animals, trees and slugs! A little bit of guided imagery will help you expand your sense of connection here. Bring back all the people you were thinking about previously: you, your friend, the neutral person and the difficult one. For example, you could imagine all of them on a bus or at a meal together. Repeat your phrases, such as, "May you all be well", "May you be loved", "May you all be happy". Then expand out to include the people living next door to you. Then imagine, in a friendly way, everyone in your street and zoom out a little to bring in your town, including the parks, your struggling football team and all the dogs and cats. The next stage is to expand further – you could imagine a map of the world with countries and oceans, to eventually visualizing the world from space. For the full enchilada you could send love and goodwill to all life forms in the universe!

Don't worry about getting the perfect image in your mind, the important thing is the effort you make in wishing every person, plant and penguin happiness.

"Put effort into wishing every person, plant and penguin happiness"

2

Positive Connection meditation: Gratitude

This is a reassuring meditation if you are feeling a bit isolated. This method reminds you that you're always interconnected with others and helps you feel grateful for their contribution to your life. Just go with it and try not to freak out.

- Sit relaxed and alert and set your timer for ten minutes. Close your eyes if that feels okay for you. Start with a simple feeling of gratitude. Maybe you can feel thankful that you are well enough to sit, or that no one is asking you to do anything for ten minutes. You could say "Thank you" silently to yourself for a few moments.

- Then remember people who have played an important part in your life. Maybe include family members, current and old friends or work colleagues you've liked. Pets, teachers or even people you haven't met but helped you in some way; artists, authors or ancestors can all become part of the cast.

"Connect with people who have played an important part in your life"

- Now imagine a sparkling fishing net that stretches over your life. The net holds all the people you're thinking about, including yourself. At a cross-section of the net, visualize one of the people you're grateful for. See their face or get a sense of their personality. Get in touch with your feelings of gratitude and connection towards them and appreciate their contribution. Then see another person at the next cross section of the net and repeat the process. Don't get too hung up about trying to remember everyone that's contributed or missing anyone out. Your dog could be in there. Recall what they have done for you – and radiate waves of appreciation and respect back. If it helps, perhaps you can visualize the good vibes as a colour travelling through the luminous net.

- The focus here is on the kindness you've received and returning the good energy. Be generous and feel glad of the connections. Stop when your timer goes off.

3

Positive Connection meditation:
Being kind to yourself

"Even suggesting that you're not a deeply terrible person can be a little disquieting"

Hold onto your didgeridoo – this meditation asks you to focus on your good points! If this makes you want to bolt for the door, you're in good company. We're all hyper-critical of ourselves. It's so hard-wired that even suggesting you're not a deeply terrible person can be a little disquieting.

"Perhaps you graciously ignored your partner's bad mood this morning"

Acknowledging that you occasionally do nice things can balance out the shed-load of mean and unpleasant stuff you say to yourself all the time. The aim here is to have a rounder, more integrated picture of yourself. The kind actions you're going to remind yourself of don't have to be heroic. It can be when you made someone laugh, watered the plants at work or when you were patient with the really slow man in the store. Perhaps you graciously ignored your partner's bad mood this morning . . . or it could be just acknowledging that you're a good listener.

You will be alternating between focusing on your small good deeds and feeling your breath coming in and out. If paying attention to your breath makes you feel tense, focus on the feeling in your hands or listen to external sounds.

- Set your timer for eight minutes. Take a few deep breaths and close your eyes.

- **_Nice things you did (two minutes)_**
  Think back and pick out a specific incident where you were nice to someone. Open up to the feeling that you did something kind. Resist the tendency to diminish or argue with it. Stay with that feeling for two minutes. If your focus wavers, just come back to remembering the good deed and let it be there.

- **Focus on your breath (two minutes)**
  Now concentrate on your in-breath then your out-breath. Try to enjoy the sensations, noticing everything about them. When you get distracted, just gently come back to your breath.

- **Nice things you did (two minutes)**
  Now go back to thinking about your kind acts and acknowledge them again. Stay with that feeling. If your mind wanders off, let go of whatever you were imagining and go back the positive feeling about yourself.

- **Focus on your breath (two minutes)**
  Return to concentrating on your breath, following all the sensations as you breathe in and out, bringing yourself back if your mind wanders off. When your timer sounds, you're all done – you lovely person, you!

"It's worth attempting meditations that don't immediately appeal because the results can be surprising"

Alternating between Single Focus and Positive Connection

Positive Connection and Single Focus meditation work well together because they offer a pleasing combination of focus, clarity and compassion. You don't have to do both in one session, alternative days would be fine. It is worth attempting meditations that don't immediately appeal because the results can often surprise you.

CHAPTER 4

Dealing With What Comes Up,
Or: I Can't Stop Thinking
About Chickens

"Usually it's about wanting something different."

Sometimes meditation can get tricky

In this chapter we look at how to cope with all the stuff that actually happens when you meditate, rather than the seductive Zen-like calm promised by other meditation books. We steer you through dealing with the more challenging and enigmatic aspects of meditation, including what to do if, for example, you find yourself bewilderingly angry or if you're obsessively worried about the dwindling dog food situation in your apartment.

Dealing with difficult emotions

Some people hope that meditation will allow them to escape from their feelings entirely, imagining they will always feel calm or so removed that they don't feel anything at all. This probably won't happen to you. Acknowledging your emotions in meditation is an essential part of the process. You're practising how to deal with them in meditation, so you understand them better in real life.

Meditation often brings up strong feelings. This is because when you're not so distracted by your thinking, you sometimes tap into underlying emotions that all that thinking was covering up. Anger from this morning's meeting, painful memories and years-old resentments can all claw their way into your awareness. We tend to judge ourselves for having intense feelings. We avoid them, squish them or stuff them into a box because emotions like anger, jealousy or grief can feel seriously uncomfortable. The important thing is to ditch the story that's attached to the emotions – try not to think about the circumstances that might have caused them. So, if you're feeling hurt because someone betrayed your trust, do your best not to replay the events in your head but concentrate on the characteristics of the feeling itself.

"Even the Dalai Lama obsesses over bad phone calls"

When a feeling appears, make a soft mental note: 'anger', 'euphoria', 'anxiety', 'grief'. If you're unsure what the emotion is, just label it 'dunno' and let it go. If particular feelings come up with annoying frequency, don't beat yourself up about that, either. It's really normal. Be extra patient with yourself. Even the Dalai Lama obsesses over bad phone calls.

"If you're unsure what the emotion is, label it 'dunno' and let it go"

Breathe into the emotions and accept they are present. Now imagine you can create a bit of space around them. Do you notice a change? Feelings shift and transform. Meditation helps you notice that intense emotions change and aren't as solid as they sometimes feel. Even in times of grief you can have a few random moments of amusement or feel clarity in the midst of fury and sadness.

Why you need to feel it

To process your emotions, you need to fully accept them in your body, so they can burn themselves out. This means exploring them in more detail. Can you feel the emotion in your body? Where is it exactly? In your stomach, your throat or your heart? Get really interested in the emotion's characteristics. Does it have a temperature? A texture? Do you feel it in flashes? Is it boiling or flat and dark?

"There's no benefit to feeling overwhelmed if you're not ready to go there. There's no time limit"

It can take courage to be open to what's really going on with you. If it's too much, you can take the toe-in-the-water approach. You can retreat and steady yourself by focusing on your breathing, or the sounds you hear. Stay there until you feel ready to go back to the emotion. Treat yourself kindly with this and be gentle and try it again when you feel steadier. Trust yourself. You'll know when and how to tackle the tricky stuff – there's no benefit to feeling overwhelmed if you're not ready to go there, and there's no time limit.

> "Sometimes the additional thoughts and emotions are harder to bear than the pain itself"

Physical pain

Pain will probably wander into your meditation on some level. Itches, twinges and aches may show up in your sessions. You might get uncomfortable while sitting, or you could be experiencing an old knee injury. Our usual reaction to pain is to reject or medicate the symptoms but meditation trains you to lean into it instead. It won't make your pain go away, but in time meditation will help you change your response to it.

When pain flares up in meditation, first gently acknowledge that it is present. Become super-curious about the sensation in your body. What is the pain? Is it a burning, throbbing or stabbing? A flash? What would it look like if you could see it? Can you feel where it is exactly? Does it have a centre? Is the pain in one area or does it move? Where are the edges of it? Does it fluctuate? Pain is seldom solid. Even if it's consistent, there will be small changes. Try to imagine breathing into it or being kind to it at its edges. Can you sit with the pain with some friendliness?

Be patient with yourself and don't take on too much. Try it in small chunks if that's easier. If the pain is too much, maybe retreat to watching your breath or steady yourself by moving your attention to sounds for a while. Being open to pain isn't easy, so be gentle when you're exploring its boundaries.

Pain add-ons

Sometimes it's not the actual sensation of pain that creates problems, but the emotions evoked by it. Pain add-ons can make the experience more difficult. For example, you might have an old injury flare up and feel resentful of the time it has robbed you. Perhaps you fear an illness will get worse and cause you to lose your job, or that your pain will eventually become intolerable. Sometimes, the additional thinking and emotions are harder to bear than the actual pain itself. You can ask yourself, "What story do I need to let go of here?" Meditation stops you spinning out and encourages you to stay with the actual sensations. Remember that once you have experienced something, you have already coped with it.

Whatever

"Okay so I'm following my breathing, big deal." Uh oh, you're bored. You might ask yourself why you're even bothering. You start to feel restless, squirm and want something, anything to break the monotony. The antidote is to make your boredom the object of your meditation. If you're using your breath as an anchor, zoom in on where you're feeling uncomfortable. How do you know you're bored? You don't usually feel boredom in your feet, so where is it? Does it move around? Become fascinated by your boredom and it will disappear.

"By now you'll be wondering whether tantric yoga might be more fun than meditating"

Bad case of doubt

A subtle, whispering troublemaker, doubt loves to undermine you. If you've got a bad case of doubt in your session, you might be wondering if tantric yoga would be more fun or even thinking you're wasting your time altogether. Doubt tries to make you give up before you've given it a chance to work. It's a common state of mind that can be difficult to spot. There is nothing wrong with healthy scepticism or questioning but doubt is different, and, left to fester, it can be corrosive. If you're in the doubt headspace you need to act – offer the monkey on your back a banana. Re-read inspiring books, remember what you get out of meditating, and maybe talk to other meditators or a teacher. Like everything else, doubt is temporary, so look it in the eye, hold your nerve and carry on.

OVERTHINKING

Here's a classic Buddhist story that describes some of the unnecessary pain you inflict on yourself by overthinking: A man is shot with an arrow, but before he allows anyone to take it out he wants to know who shot the arrow, why he shot it, what type of arrow it was, what sort of material it's made from and what the long-term implications of the removal will be. Buddhists suggest you just take out the arrow.

Mental noting

'Noting' is where you gently describe whatever you find distracting in your meditation. This could be anything from: 'thinking', 'boredom', 'itching' and 'guilt' to 'hungry', 'angry' or 'noise'. When you have labelled the thought, recognize it, then let it go and continue with following your breath or return to your anchor. 'Thinking' will come up so often that breaking it down into categories such as 'worrying', 'planning' or 'remembering' will help you identify some of your patterns and give you a little more insight.

"Realizing how easily you get abducted by your thoughts can come as a bit of a shock"

Don't too spend too much time obsessing over which category your thoughts fit into. If it's taking too much time to work it out, just lump it all into 'thinking' and drop it. Popping yourself out of the content of the thoughts and observing that you got side-tracked is the point of the exercise. Watch the tone of voice in your head when labelling your thoughts and try for a quiet, friendly tone.

Realizing how easily you get abducted by thoughts can come as a bit of a shock, but it is actually progress because now you can see how much unhelpful thinking is going on in there. In time, you may notice recurring patterns and your favourite neurosis will become clear.

A LITTLE BUFFER

You can learn so much about yourself from how you deal with your feelings. The more aware you are of what's going on emotionally, the easier it will be when you're in the next situation that makes you want to set fire to your own hair. Meditation gives you space to pause before you react. Maybe not every time, but it's encouraging when you notice that you're managing your emotions a bit better.

"One way of handling upsetting recurring thoughts is to give them a nickname"

The joy of naming your neuroses

Becoming more aware of what's annoying you isn't always fun, but it is actually giving you a very useful opportunity to deal with what's causing you pain. One way of handling upsetting thought patterns is to give them a nickname. Make it funny, something that punctures the intensity of the feeling. If you're habitually thinking your career is doomed, your neurosis could be Unemployable Ed. Or, if you're beating yourself up for procrastinating, perhaps Deadline Dodger has popped up.

> "Make friends with your neuroses – see them as quirks rather than tragic flaws"

Keeping the names amusing helps put that imagined dark part of yourself into some perspective and takes some of its power away. Make friends with your neuroses – see them as quirks rather than tragic flaws. These hurtful ideas you have about yourself will lose their potency if you can just allow them to exist. Look your monsters in the eye and one day you'll even be able to laugh at them. Everyone has their stuff to deal with – everyone! So next time Jealous Gilbert hijacks your otherwise pleasant day, you can acknowledge him, poke fun at his insecurities and then in a firm but friendly manner, escort him on his way. If you've been repeating these patterns for years it might take some work, but you're getting more skilled at it every time you meditate.

Kill The Worry Loop

Let's say you wake up thinking about your presentation for work. A bit of worrying will help you do a good job, but after 18 obsessive thought loops, it stops being useful. Next time you catch yourself in a worry loop, note 'worrying' and drop it. And get on with your day. Now, this isn't saying that it won't come up again, but it gives you the skill of being able to recognize and bin unhelpful repetitive crap in your head. Cool, isn't it?

Desire

You are a bottomless pit of wanting. You lust after all kinds of stuff because it makes you feel good, at least for a while: donuts, praise, Instagram hits, booze. You can also desire more of what you already have, such as wishing an evening would never end. Desire has a dodgy reputation in some meditation circles, like it's something you can extinguish or should feel guilty about. But it's one of life's greatest driving forces. Getting what you want can feel wonderful, but being stuck in desire can get you into some dark places. Addiction, chronic restlessness or continual dissatisfaction are signs that your desire has you in its clutches.

"Who thinks, 'Fine. I've had all the admiration I need for now'?"

Desire is hard to regulate because the line between wanting to satisfy your basic needs and craving much more is wire thin. And you never really feel satisfied for long. Who thinks, "Fine. I've had all the admiration I need for now"? To get what you crave you have to manipulate the outside world into giving it to you, but you're never completely satisfied with the results. Your restless animal mind tries to convince you that X will supply the fulfilment you seek. But, of course, that never happens because humans are not built to be content. You were built to survive.

If you're happy in the present moment, you don't need to control where your validation comes from. Desire arises when you believe that what you have now isn't enough. Meditation can bring awareness and more control over your cravings and ambitions. It will be easier to see what's behind your desires. Usually it's about wanting something different. Learning to be content with what's happening right now shows you already have what you need to be happy.

Quench your desire with RAIN

To deal with desire, or any tricky emotion, you can try this catchy little RAIN acronym. You're thinking we're going to recommend you listen to enchanting sounds of the rainforest now, aren't you? No. RAIN is a bit more pragmatic than that:

R – Recognize the presence of desire. For instance, if you've been fantasizing about the woman you have a secret crush on finally realizing how irresistible you are – that's a great start! It's always helpful to see what your mind is up to. Make a mental note of it, gently say to yourself, "desire" or "wanting Russell Crowe".

> "Gently note to yourself 'desire' or 'wanting Russell Crowe'"

A – Accept that it's okay to want something or someone. It's just a thought in your head. Don't fight or judge it.

> "It's always helpful to see what your mind is up to"

I – Investigate. Without re-starting the fantasy, think about what it feels like in your body. Where do you feel the sensations? Does it have a shape, temperature or colour? Does it build or come in waves?

"Witnessing a craving pass away can be a very powerful experience"

N – Non-Identification. Remember you're not your emotions or thoughts. By noticing the desire, you can separate yourself slightly from it. Let it exist but don't give it more fuel. All desires come and go. Give it time, watch it and let it pass. Witnessing a craving pass away can be a very powerful experience.

"Remember you're not your emotions or thoughts"

Difficult times

Anyone who meditates regularly will go through a tough patch. Maybe you're experiencing a stressful time at work, you're ill or someone close to you has died. Meditation itself can raise challenging stuff. It's a hugely rewarding activity, but it can also feel like the last thing you want to do. For anyone going through a difficult phase it's essential you are kind to yourself. If meditation teaches you anything, it should teach you that. Allow yourself to feel terrible. If you feel anxious for months, then that's how it is. Give yourself the time you need to feel better.

Make sure your meditation routine isn't adding to your woes. If sitting on a chair is too much, lie on the floor. It's okay if you fall asleep – you probably needed it. Try walking meditation when you're struggling with sitting still. And if you want to sob your eyes out – go ahead!

"Feel what you feel, don't fight it and don't judge it"

Feel what you feel, don't fight it and don't judge it. Acknowledge your pain and breathe through it. You should always be friendly to yourself while meditating. You can take that quite literally by imagining how a friend would behave towards you if you were having a difficult time. Take that person's advice and be super nice to yourself.

There's always additional help if you need it. This could be from a meditation teacher, group or a counsellor. The Positive Connection meditations in Chapter 3 are very helpful when things get challenging. If you're not using them already, add a few minutes to your usual session and see how it goes. Sometimes these dark places can be the catalysts that change your life for the better – even though it doesn't feel like it at the time! When your life is full of change and uncertainty, meditation can help you stay present and focused.

Forcing yourself to relax

We tend to approach meditation with the same attitude we give other activities in our life. You want to achieve something, so you invest a great deal of effort and strive for a goal. If you're trying too hard to meditate, you may have a clenched jaw, or hunched shoulders or get frustrated and want to give up. If you feel more agitated at the end of your session than when you started, you might be falling into this trap.

"Having set goals might be working against you and making your meditation experience a bit grim"

It's natural that you want something out of meditation, otherwise you wouldn't bother doing it. But having set goals and ambitions might be working against you. It can also make your experience of meditation a bit grim.

Unclench a little and listen. No, seriously, take a moment and listen to the noise in the room. No huge effort, no straining to identify the softest sound, just direct your attention to what you can hear. That is the amount of effort that is needed to meditate, moment after moment. Anything more than that will be making you uptight and unhappy. Lighten up, it's not an exam!

Gleeful squeaks

Meditation trains your mind to find subtle pleasure and can produce surprising moments of delight. During your practice you may enjoy waves of contentment or calmness to feeling downright chirpy. Gentle tingling in your scalp or a warmth in your hands is a good sign that you're tuned into your body and the present moment. Smiling when you meditate can create unexpectedly happy feelings, even if you're only smiling because you feel one step away from suggesting a group hug at the office. Fears and worries almost always live in the past or future. Your life is happening in one constant now – and you're the only one in control of what you're paying attention to. You're training yourself to notice the nice things in your life. This could be anything from enjoying slicing up mushrooms to realizing you're finally ready to forgive your ex.

> "You're one step away from suggesting a group hug in the office"

CHAPTER 5

The Only Way to Reap the Rewards of Meditation is to Actually Do Some

"Waiting on inspiration is a clever excuse not to meditate!"

Eventually, meditation will become just what you do

Having a routine you look forward to means you don't have to summon up extra willpower or waste time finding ingenious excuses to avoid it.

> "If you frequently think bitter thoughts about the past, you'll get quite good at it"

Your habits form your default mode for living. This is a wonderful thing because you don't want to spend energy thinking about how you put your socks on in the morning. Making habits work for you is important because, in the long term, you become what you do most often. This also applies to your mental habits. If you frequently think bitter thoughts about the past, you'll get quite good at it. If you spend years kicking yourself for not being good enough, you will become an expert at it.

You might feel you're faced with a plethora of daily choices, but in truth a hefty 40% of your activities – from the food you order, the route you take to work and who you feel comfortable talking to at parties – are handled by your automatic pilot. When meditation becomes a habit, it will require less effort because it will just be part of your life.

YOUR MiND iS GROOVY

Imagine your mind is a rock and your thoughts are like water running over it. In time, the water creates small channels in the rock and flows easily through these grooves. If you've spent loads of time worrying, then your 'How-to-worry' groove gradually gets bigger. This is why life-time habits are difficult to conquer. You become so comfortable with worrying that any challenging situations slip easily into the worry groove because it's second nature. But you can change this. Meditation makes you notice your favourite grooves and helps you create different ones.

Enjoy it, it's not a chore

Even if you understand on an intellectual level that meditation is good for you, you won't keep doing it unless you're getting something out of it. It makes sense then to pick the type of meditation that makes you feel good. Does walking meditation appeal? Make it a regular thing and focus on finding pleasure in it. You're meditating to feel happier, kinder and more focused, not because the Dalai Lama will be impressed. The only way to get to the good stuff is to crack on with it.

"Don't spend 15 minutes fiddling with chairs, apps and timers"

Planning how you'll meditate is useful. Thinking about where, when and for how long will cement the idea in that fidgety mind of yours. Spend a few moments setting up a timer on your phone and get your cushion plumped up ready for action. Have it all set up, so you don't spend 15 minutes fiddling with chairs, apps and timers.

There's (almost) always a way

Finding time can be tricky but even when your day is stuffed with activity you will be able to squeeze in a quick session. Perhaps you can sit in your car for three minutes before going into your house or the journey between meetings can transformed into a walking meditation. We think of these activities as blank bits, or gaps between more important things. It is rewarding to reclaim these little spaces for yourself. This is where mindfulness, which we talked about on page 13, comes into its own.   Even in stressful situations, mindful moments create calming little pools of awareness. Much like appreciating the bear's velvety fur before it tears your face off.

> "There will be times when your meditation routine will be rudely kicked out the window"

Have a back-up plan. There will be times when your pleasant meditation routine will be rudely kicked out the window. A week-long crisis at work or a child's illness can mean you really don't have two minutes to spare. In this situation, first be kind to yourself, and second, see if you can keep a connection to your practice. Instead of your usual sitting, you could bring your focused attention to whatever you are doing. For example, when washing your hands, give it your full attention. Feel the water on your skin, notice the smell of the soap, look at the rainbows in the bubbles and then listen to the water gurgling down the sink. These small sanctuaries can be sanity-saving when everything else has descended into madness.

WHAT ARE YOU GETTING OUT OF THIS?

If you spent three hours at the gym you want to see stronger triceps, so it's reasonable to expect to feel happier after three hours of meditation. But meditation is unlike any other activity. We meditate to observe and understand ourselves better. What you get out of it might be quite subtle and the insights will arrive in their own time, without pushing. Try to avoid the pumping-iron mentality.

Reminders, bribes and cattle-prods

In the same way that runners put their trainers out to remind them to go for a run, you can create a meditation prompt. A 'just breathe' Post-It on your car dashboard, a favourite blanket near where you meditate, the annoying radio presenter you always turn off – they can all be cues that it's time to meditate. Get it done early. Yes, even if you're not a morning person this is worth a try. Meditating before your day starts has a number of advantages. In particular, your brain isn't buzzing from work, so it may be easier to focus.

Don't set yourself up to fail. Telling yourself you're going to get up at 4am and meditate for two hours every day won't work. You might do it once, but you will probably hate it and give this book to Oxfam. Much better to commit to five enjoyable minutes every day.

Light bribery can persuade a reluctant meditator to act. Ten minutes deserves a cookie. Using scratch cards or gin as a motivator might get the job done but may drain some of your hard-earned serenity.

Emergency Fake Out meditation

"You'd rather pick out the peas from the back of the freezer than meditate"

When nothing else works and you'd rather pick out the peas from the back of the freezer than meditate, you need the 'fake out' method. This works like a charm and proves that even annoyed meditation is meditation:

- Adopt your best sulky teenager mode and drag your reluctant ass into your meditation posture.
- Cross your arms, frown and refuse to meditate.
- Focus your attention on one breath.
- Breathe in. Breathe out.
- When you get distracted, go back to your breath.
- Repeat for ten breaths.

"In a hyper-distracted world, meditation is a radical act"

IT TAKES BALLS

In Buddhist traditions meditation is often called The Way of the Warrior because it takes balls to look at yourself with honesty and kindness. It is much easier to say that you are a 'type A' personality or Scottish, or "My mum was a worrier, too" than accept you are not happy with yourself and want to change. Most people feel disquieted at the thought of being with their own mind for more than a few minutes. In a hyper-distracted world, meditation is a radical act.

Groups, teachers and apps

Waiting on inspiration is a clever excuse not to meditate! The best way to stay enthused is to do the thing. One of the most effective ways to make you meditate (as opposed to just reading books on it!) is to join a class or group. You'll quickly discover you're not the only easily distracted person in the room. Most beginners' classes don't need commitment. It's also an engaging way of trying out different methods and teaching styles. Check out the organizations listed in the resources at the back of the book.

If you can't get to a class in person, there are various online groups where the slight pressure of knowing that other people are meditating can be enough to get you to join in. There's something a little magical about connecting with people in cyberspace, thousands of miles apart and in different time zones, logging in from their devices to sit in contemplation together.

Creating an instant messaging group with the people you've met in the online group, where you can share your experiences and compare notes, could also help you feel connected, as will finding an encouraging friend who also wants to make it a daily habit.

Seek out great teachers. Talking with someone with vast experience can be a gamechanger and open areas that you weren't even aware of. Every teacher has a unique approach – some will feel right instantly, others will make you cringe!

> "The biggest problem is sifting through the New Age waffle to find the good stuff"

Meditation apps are a fantastic resource. Most have guided meditations where someone talks you through the process and gives gentle reminders to keep your attention. Some apps also have timers and will even send you reminders to meditate. The biggest problem is sifting through all the New Age waffle to find the good stuff. We've selected a few that we like in the resources section at the back of the book.

GUIDED MEDITATIONS VERSUS DIY

Guided meditations, such as apps where someone gives you instructions and gentle reminders to keep your attention, are very helpful. It is shocking just how quickly you forget that you're supposed to be meditating! Others find this type of instruction intrusive and prefer their own method. One isn't better than the other and it's fine to do both. Whatever gets you to meditate is good.

Still not meditating?

You've read the book, you totally understand why meditation helps and yet, mysteriously, you're still not doing any. Perhaps the thought of spending a few moments in your own head freaks you out a bit. Although we are thinking machines, the thought of paying careful attention to this process can be daunting.

Relaxing with the mess in there is what it's all about! But if the idea of having a look at your own thoughts is really horrifying, you might want to talk it through with a counsellor.

"Worrying that you'll become too happy or calm is a brilliant example of how your mind can turn anything into a problem"

Some people worry they might get too happy and calm if they really get into meditation. This is a brilliant example of how our brains can turn anything into a problem. But it also shows that you can be oddly attached to your worries. If "I'm a worrier" is very much part of who you think you are or if it's the glue that keeps your life together, the loss of that can feel threatening.

Thankfully, the benefits of meditation are gradual so any increase in happiness can be accommodated slowly without too much upset. Another concern some have is that you might lose your 'edge' or become a bit passive because meditation encourages you to accept what is happening. The reverse is usually the case because the practice helps you respond, rather than react, to situations, which means you actually have more resources to manage your life.

"Just meditate for two minutes – make the bar so low you trip over it"

Perhaps you have completely fallen off the wagon. Despite your best intentions you've not meditated in months or even years. It's normal to have some ups and downs when establishing a regular routine. The art of meditation is starting again. You've not lost anything. Find a style you find enjoyable and meditate for two minutes. Make the bar so low you trip over it. Haphazard meditation is better than no meditation at all. Welcome back!

NOT VERY ZEN

If you mention to friends that you're trying meditation you might be met with "Oooh, it's all a bit Zen" comments and jokes about the sound of one hand clapping. If you know any martial arts moves this would be an appropriate time to show what you can do. If not, smile and nod. They will get bored eventually.

For those who are interested, Zen is a form of Buddhism practised in China, Japan, Korea and Vietnam. Zazen is the Zen name for sitting meditation. Traditionally, Zazen has a more formal approach to posture and very broadly consists of three techniques: Concentration, Koan Introspection (the use of skilful questions to deepen understanding) and Shikantaz (just sitting).

The path to enlightenment (just kidding!)

blah, blah.... meditation... blaaaaaah!

So, you're meditating contentedly and are increasingly interested and pleased with the benefits of your new routine ... or you've just skipped to the back of the book! Once you've got the basics under your belt there are a number of ways to develop it further.

"You'd rather stick pins in your eyeballs than try a Positive Connection meditation"

Change the scenery. Meditating in your local park or even in the cupboard under the stairs can be refreshing. If ten minutes feels easy enough, up it by a few minutes each session and see how it goes. It can be interesting and challenging to try one of the methods that you took an instant dislike to. If you'd rather stick pins in your eyeballs than try a Positive Connection meditation, there could be some revealing insights for you there. See it as playing, rather than a 'do-it-cos-you-should' activity.

Really enjoying it or want to deepen your experience quickly? It might be time to go on a retreat. Usually run by meditation schools or teachers, retreats are an excellent opportunity to explore in a supportive environment. Retreats give you a break from your usual routine and can last anything from one or two days to three months. A day or weekend retreat can give you a taste of what to expect and are often aimed at beginners.

DON'T GET TOO PREACHY

When you get excited about meditation you may be tempted to recommend it to everyone in your life. This is probably wildly irritating. Dropping not-so-subtle hints about how you think meditation might help your friends is going to backfire. Yes, if someone asks you why you are calmer and happier you can tell them about your new passion. But let them ask first. Evangelizers tend not to get invited to parties.

"The first time you stop yourself spiralling into negative self-chat is meditation gold"

Good luck!

Meditation is not a magic solution for all problems. But realizing that your mind won't shut up is the first step to managing it better. The first time you stop yourself spiralling into negative self-chat or notice you feel calmer is meditation gold. That's because you're showing yourself that change is possible.

Your life amounts to what you focus on, so we're privileged that you gave us your precious attention, even if you just looked at the pictures!

Say hello and let us know how you're getting on at our website: www.mymindwontshutup.com.

Twitter:
My Mind Won't Shut Up!
@shut_up_my_mind

Facebook:
facebook.com/mymindwontshutup

Instagram:
My Mind Won't Shut Up!
@mindwontshutup

RESOURCES

Some apps, books, organizations and websites that we really like or have referenced in the book:

Apps

10% Happier – www.10percenthappier.com

Calm – www.calm.com

Headspace – www.headspace.com

Insight Timer – www.insighttimer.com

Waking Up – www.wakingup.com

Books

10% Happier: How I Tamed the Voice in My Head, Reduced Stress Without Losing My Edge, and Found Self-Help That Actually Works – A True Story, Dan Harris (Yellow Kite, 2014).

Advice Not Given, Dr Mark Epstein (Hay House, 2018).

Full Catastrophe Living, Jon Kabat-Zinn (Piatkus, 1990).

The 4-Hour Work Week: Escape 9–5, Live Anywhere, and Join the New Rich, Tim Ferriss (Crown Publishing Group, 2007).

The Power of Habit: Why We Do What We Do, and How to Change, Charles Duhigg (Random House, 2012).

The Science of Meditation: How to Change Your Brain, Mind and Body, Daniel Goldman & Richard Davidson (Penguin 2017).

Waking Up: Searching for Spirituality Without Religion, Sam Harris (Simon & Schuster, 2014).

Organizations

Breathworks – www.breathworks-mindfulness.org.uk
Counselling/Therapy links – www.rscpp.co.uk
School of Life – www.theschooloflife.com
Triratna Buddhist Organization – www.thebuddhistcentre.com

Websites/Podcasts

Dharma seed – www.dharmaseed.org
Meet up – www.meetup.com
Russell Brand, Under The Skin – www.russellbrand.com/podcast/

TriggerHub.org is one of the most elite and scientifically proven forms of mental health intervention

Trigger Publishing is the leading independent mental health and wellbeing publisher in the UK and US. Clinical and scientific research conducted by assistant professor Dr Kristin Kosyluk and her highly acclaimed team in the Department of Mental Health Law & Policy at the University of South Florida (USF), as well as complementary research by her peers across the US, has independently verified the power of lived experience as a core component in achieving mental health prosperity. Specifically, the lived experiences contained within our bibliotherapeutic books are intrinsic elements in reducing stigma, making those with poor mental health feel less alone, providing the privacy they need to heal, ensuring they know the essential steps to kick-start their own journeys to recovery, and providing hope and inspiration when they need it most.

Delivered through TriggerHub, our unique online portal and accompanying smartphone app, we make our library of bibliotherapeutic titles and other vital resources accessible to individuals and organizations anywhere, at any time and with complete privacy, a crucial element of recovery. As such, TriggerHub is the primary recommendation across the UK and US for the delivery of lived experiences.

At Trigger Publishing and TriggerHub, we proudly lead the way in making the unseen become seen. We are dedicated to humanizing mental health, breaking stigma and challenging outdated societal values to create real action and impact. Find out more about our world-leading work with lived experience and bibliotherapy via triggerhub.org, or by joining us on:

🐦 @triggerhub_

ⓕ @triggerhub.org

📷 @triggerhub_